Illustrated

by
Tony Benford

1

Copyright

Note from the Author

Dear Reader

The Lord is always faithful. He's always near. He cares deeply about every detail of your life—every moment, every tear, every joy. Our confidence is anchored in His Word, which never fails. Even when it feels like nothing is changing, God is still moving. His love is constant, His presence is real, and His care is personal —for everyone, including you.

This book was written as a simple yet powerful reminder: in your best moments, Jesus cares. And in your hardest moments, He is still there. He was born for you, He walked this earth for you, He suffered and died for you—and He rose again so you can live with hope, peace, and joy.

No matter where you are or how you feel, remember this truth: Jesus cares for you. Always.

With Prayer and Thanksgiving,

Tony Benford

I know that
Jesus cares for me
I know
That
Jesus
Loves me

I know that
Jesus cares for me
I know
That
Jesus
Loves me

I know
That
Jesus cares
For me

He came to see about
Me
When nobody was
There
For me

He took away
My pain
So my life
Would
Be
spared

He died on the cross
So His love
Could
Be
Shared

O man
Nobody like Jesus
Can
Rock
Me

He took me to the
Top
So nobody
Can
Block
Me

He put me in His hand
So nobody
Will
Drop me

I've got
The Holy Ghost
So nobody
Can
Stop me

Let's go!

I know that
Jesus cares for me
I know
That
Jesus
Loves me

I know that
Jesus cares for me
I know
That
Jesus
Loves me

My God is on
TIME
So nobody can
CLOCK
Me

The devil
Can't
See me
No
he can't even
WATCH
Me

His arms are
Too
Short
No
he can't even
Box me

I hit him with the
Word
Now they're calling
Me
ROCKY!

Everyday,
All night
My God
Is
The best

He told me
Not to
Worry
He can
Handle
The rest

He gives me
Daily bread
Yeah
It's always
So fresh

They ask me,
"How ya feeling?"
I'm too blessed
To be
Stressed

I know...

I know that
Jesus cares for me
I know
That
Jesus
Loves me

I know that
Jesus cares for me
I know
That
Jesus
Loves me

I bet you didn't know
That
We always
Win

See
Jesus came along
And
Forgave
Your
Sins

He did it
For you
But
He did it
For all
Men

That's why you see
Me
Wearing
This
Big ole grin

That's right
Jesus Christ
Is
My Lord
And
Savior

I'm carefully
Designed
By my
King
And
Creator

Remember that
You're blessed
Don't forget
Highly favored

Now run
And
Tell that
To
Your
Next door
Neighbor...

GOOD NEWS!

I know that
Jesus cares for me
I know
That
Jesus
Loves me

I know that
Jesus cares for me
I know
That
Jesus
Loves me

www.ingramcontent.com/pod-product-compliance
Lightning Source LLC
Chambersburg PA
CBHW041801040426
42447CB00005B/284